THE GREAT UNCLUTTERING

The Collected Poetry
of Carolyn Moore

Edited by Laura D. Weeks
& Justin Rigamonti

 PCC
PANTHER
PRESS

Copyright ©2022 by Portland Community College, Portland, OR

Cover design by Justin Rigamonti
Copy editing by Jessie Carver
Typsetting and page layout by Cameon Jackman

First Edition, First Printing
Published by PCC Panther Press
www.pcc.edu

For information about permission to reuse any material from this book, please contact PCC's Humanities and Arts Council at harts@pcc.edu

ISBN: 979-8-9867227-0-2

Dedicated to the family of Carolyn Moore

CONTENTS

FROM
The Last Night of Maskmaking

FROM
*Why I Won't Take My Jane Austen Action Figure
Out of Her Packaging*

Uncollected Works

FOREWORD

Justin Rigamonti

Carolyn Moore loved gardening almost more than anything else. Gardening was in her blood. In the epigraph to her poem "The Garden of Enormous Language," she points out that Olson women, on her mother's side, were "mothers of gorgeous sweat," who would "water, weed, and hoe all the hot sky long." Carolyn was proud of her earthy roots, and she kept up an apple and pear orchard, a small vineyard, and multiple gardens, all on the thirteen acres of land she retired to in the 1990s.

But despite this deep familial affinity for working the soil, Carolyn admitted in a 2010 interview with *Interrobang Magazine* what you might have already guessed: her "chief love" was poetry. "Poetry is by far the most demanding genre in which I've struggled," she says, "and therefore the most challenging and most addictive one."

As my co-editor Laura D. Weeks notes in her Introduction, Carolyn composed poetry using a method she called "composting." She would jot down thoughts, memories, and phrases, and then store them in her notebooks and computer files for weeks or months, allowing them to gestate. Even the work she did to support her "addiction"—the twenty years of teaching at Humboldt State University in Arcata, California, as well as her side hustle researching and editing "passages for comprehension tests . . . for subjects ranging from ionic soil stabilizers to the history of the toothbrush"—served as a means of gathering phrases, hoarding them. She would then draw from these notes and organize what she gleaned, taming the wildness of language into iambic rows. She called it "wrestling words to the paper mat," and one imagines an Olson woman, wrist-deep in pungent loam, alchemizing yesterday's dead into furrows of new life.

Her poems usually began in blank verse, unrhymed iambic pentameter, but once a poem was ironed out on the page, Carolyn would put it through a rigorous "free verse diet" to help "weed out phrases and words that function as unnecessary filler." And this cycle of gathering and trimming, hoarding then releasing, cluttering and decluttering, wasn't just a hallmark of her poetic process. It was a constant theme within her work as well.

In the poem "Instructions for Fall Cleaning," she writes:

> Fall's for tackling clutter. June rehearsed
> you for this task. When you deadhead a rose,
> you make your cut above a five-leafed twig
> and trust this paradox: prune to increase.

She thrived in this paradoxical gathering of language and experience—notching trips to Greece, England, and the Shetland Islands—only to sift through them on the creative page, finding the gold in the ore.

There's a meditation on this metaphor in the last poem of her last published work, the prize-winning collection *What Euclid's Third Axiom Neglects to Mention about Circles*. The poem is called "Botany, Domestic Architecture, and the End of Days," and it begins with a leaf skeleton, the remains of a camellia leaf at the end of its life cycle, having fallen to the ground. "Larvae strip the leaf to an elegant theory / of itself," she writes. The poem suggests this stripping down is a model we can follow:

> Likewise, the family house must cast off doors.
> Drawers must pull out, flip over, and shed their hoards:
> the tarnished baby spoon and sugar tongs,
> half-used candles, lids to long-gone jars

And why should we undergo this "Great Uncluttering," as she called it in the title of an unfinished manuscript? Her answer is simple: "To carry off / what never should be saved." Every life must be, one day, folded under the soil, with only the gold winnowed out for the next generation, and so to live well is to practice this gathering and letting go.

Which is what Carolyn Moore did. She lived a generous life, cluttered with joy—as teacher, writer, traveler, and aunt—and from that largesse, she extracted a beautiful, refined legacy. Not only in the gift of her gorgeous home and acreage to Portland Community College, now the site of the Carolyn Moore Writing Residency, but also in the wisdom she distilled in her poems.

What a privilege then to gather her finest work together for you into one volume. Carolyn was as prolific in writing as she was in all of her life ventures, and to create this collection, Laura and I sifted through many published and prize-winning poems, as well as file after file of uncollected work, much of which is published here for the first time. Our hope for this book is that it continues Carolyn's legacy of illumination, of gathering and winnowing, of making room in the heart for new life.

"The goal is rapture," Carolyn writes. "The means? Ravish, devour. / All that remains will let through light at last."

INTRODUCTION

The Many Voices of Carolyn Moore

Laura D. Weeks

We met on the most inauspicious of dates. It was 9/11, and members of the newly formed Portlandia writing group telephoned back and forth, nervously feeling each other's pulse as to whether we should meet. We did, and for Carolyn Moore and myself, it led to a fast and fruitful friendship spanning many years, many workshops, and more than one re-formation of the original group.

Moore's writing habits were idiosyncratic in both senses: writing as penmanship and as creation. I have before me the detached, semi-printed letters of her signature, the enormous capital "C" curling protectively around the letters of her name. More mosaic than cursive, her handwriting had not a ligature in sight. Moore was born left-handed, and, as was common practice at that time, was forced to write right-handed. The result was, predictably, disaster.

> "Longhand is a prison sentence from which I cannot escape, through which words and thoughts tunnel out and are lost forever." (From an interview given in 2010 for the journal *Interrobang*.)

Ultimately, the computer keyboard was her salvation, but it was never the urgrund of her creative process. That distinction belonged to her notebooks. Rarely in our writing sessions did a poem emerge fully fleshed. (Two notable exceptions are "How to Housebreak a Shadow" and "Two Conversations in a White, White Kitchen.") Instead, she filled her notebooks with jottings, phrases, themes, ideas, which she then lay aside to "compost," as she called it.

In christening her notebooks "compost," she declared her affinity for soil, at the same time providing a clue to her creative process. The act of "tunneling" in the quote above is an apt metaphor for her art: a process of unearthing that which is "underground and out of sight."

"Yes to worm, mole, all burrowers who nudge, / snuffle, and ruck what surface-dwellers miss." ("Lars Poetica's Guidelines for Nominating the Next King of Beasts")

Moore was a consummate gardener, delighting in both the labor and the language of botany. But the act of working the soil had a darker aspect as well, as we see in an early version of "Winter Solstice in London," where she buys a potato "smelling of the earth's armpit."

The potato smells of harrowing,
of distressing the soil in the faith
such pain will bring relief.

Gardening, then, is both unearthing that which lies hidden in the unconscious, and a form of exorcism. Moore, like her grandmother, "trusted potatoes to tunnel her way out of any darkness."

To some readers, especially in the context of contemporary lyric, Moore's poetry may seem brilliant but dry. It is unequivocally devoid of sentimentality, tending more towards intellect than affect. Her much-loved John Frederick Nims (her copy of his *Western Wind* is worn and split into three pieces, despite several generations of tape) warns poets against sentimentality:

> Healthy emotion is object-directed; sentimentality is
> subject-directed. . . . The sentimentalist is less concerned
> with the object of his emotion than with the fact that he
> himself is feeling it. The sentimentalist hallucinates, turns
> the world into a warm nest in which he can coddle his own
> snug feelings. He sees only so much of reality as confirms
> him in his enjoyment of the more tender and tearful
> emotions. (John Frederick Nims, *Western Wind*, p. 128.)

Sentimentality is self-oriented, and Moore distrusted it. Above all, she distrusted the poet's overweening "I."

> In the '90s I found myself squirming through too many
> poetry readings comprised of an unvaried litany of
> quasi-confessional or otherwise lyric poems. All that
> *I, me, mine* seemed so self-involved. (*Interrobang*)

In her efforts to circumvent the "I," she employs a dizzying array of tactics. First, the use of plural pronouns: in cases where the reader expects the first person singular, we encounter the first person plural "we," "us." Even more frequently, we encounter the second person plural: the "you" of direct address. "Trios are safer," Moore remarked in an unpublished poem, and it is telling that even at her most confessional, in "Two Conversations in a White, White Kitchen," there are THREE people in the room (the father, the daughter, and the dead mother for whom she fills a coffee mug).

Secondly, Moore indulges in her own peculiar form of praeteritio, often accomplished via references to geology and geography. Scarred, scared, and contemplating divorce, she circumvents the emotional: "We'll take the safe / route and handle this through travelogue." ("Searching Tucson for Words to Say Goodbye"). Likewise, in "Like Photos the Dead Woman Forgot to Date" she claims, "Last night I lost Poros." Then she proceeds to resurrect it, stone on stone.

Her primary strategy, however, lies on speaking through other voices. Often this takes the form of epistolary or quasi-epistolary poems. Her grandmother writes to her in London. Frau Karl Marx writes to her brother asking for money. A transplanted midwestern farm wife writes to her friend in Dakota. A mother writes to acknowledge her daughter's gift. Each voice allows the self to slide behind another's turn of phrase.

In adopting other voices, her preferred genre was the mask or persona poem, and it is here she demonstrates the full range of her genius. The words *mask* and *persona* are interchangeable, inasmuch as "persona" originally meant the mask worn by an actor in ancient Greek drama to designate the role being played. In Moore's world, everything—things animate and inanimate, creatures natural and mythical—everything found its voice.

> A persona poem frees us to consider the Other. . . . I have serious poems spoken by a toadstool, a ceramic cup, a music dictionary, an apple (THE apple speaking to Eve), a multiple-choice quiz and vinegar. (*Interrobang*)

Maintaining the voice of the Other in a persona poem is a bit of a two-edged sword. While the poet's "I" is never entirely eclipsed (witness the vitriol bubbling barely below the surface in "The Toadstool Blames His Victim"), the mask can be held at a greater or lesser distance from the "I." Too great a distance, and the mask lacks conviction. Too close, and the self risks being absorbed by the mask. In the quote above, Moore considers the persona poem objectively, as an excursion into the mind of the Other. It is also a form of protection. It is in fact the last line of defense in the struggle between the self and the Other.

The protective function of the mask is brought into terrifying focus by Rilke in his *Notebooks of Malte Laurids Brigge*. He begins with the simple observation that we all wear many masks in our life. ("There are quantities of human beings, but there are many more faces, for each person has several. There are people who wear the same face for years.") He concludes with the horrible vision of the naked, flayed self.

> But the woman, the woman. She had completely collapsed into herself, forward into her hands.
> The street was too empty . . . it caught my step from under my feet and clattered about with it hither and yon, as with a wooden clog. The woman startled and pulled away too quickly out of herself, too violently, so that her face remained in her hands. I could see it lying in them, its hollow form. It cost me indescribable effort to stay with those hands and not to look at what had torn itself out of them. I shuddered to see a face from the inside, but still I was much more afraid of the naked flayed head without a face. (Rilke, 1992, p. 16.)

A similar process unfolds in Moore's poem "The Cul-de-Sac's Crone Reproaches Her Neighbor with Quince." It begins with her trademark "tripod" structure: the unnamed male ("his voice"), the mask/persona (the crone) and the poet's "I," here reduced to "yours," "you."

> Look—I've had enough. These nights, his voice
> slams yours to the mat. Yours, the smaller
> wrestler in the wrong weight class, lies there
> so still, I count your pocks of silence
> in fear they will add up to zero.

The real magic of transformation occurs in stanza two, where the mask takes on a life of its own. Through the well-worn agency of a mirror, it insinuates itself, covering and obliterating the self.

> Last night I dreamed I slipped over you,
> a second skin. You looked up startled
> from brushing your teeth—and there we were,
> joined tight in your mirror. Your wet fingers
> traced my cheek, worn as the leather purse
>
> that could hold all you need for leaving.

In the fourth stanza the poet's "I" pulls away from the mask, producing the same terrifying effect as in the Rilke excerpt above: the exposure of the injured, vulnerable self.

> You tugged the shell of my nose from yours.
> The holy pain of separation!
> You peeled off my face. The rest of me
> puddled at your feet. . . .

The poem ends on a note of hope. The self takes refuge in the image of a quail first sheltering, then taking flight, birds being a well-established Jungian symbol for the soul.

From the cul-de-sac crone to the climbing clematis, from termites to toadstools, Moore trains our untutored ears to hear the marvelous voices of the universe. Some are lofty (the mermaid, the muse); some are so humble they may have escaped our notice (the bickering of ice cubes in a drink, the "muffled shrieks of bussed, abandoned plates"). Together they embrace us in a chorus of trust:

> Mother, if you can hear me—please know this:
> I trust in voices. I'll take them any color.

FROM

The Flavors
of Quarks and Blame

The Refined Savage Press, 2008

Saucers are not permitted in the classroom,
where we align our handles facing east
after the first bell. No clinking during lecture.

Your first assignment requires you stretch
out of the Self. We best achieve this feat
through empathy with matter opposite
from our own. By nature we are hard—and so
we'll study . . . soft. For subjects, choose from these:

> *the inner life of textiles, or*
> *butter: its use and abuse, or*
> *the secret schemes of loam.*

You're not required to believe your thoughts—not once
you've turned them in. You may return to Self
in the final paper on genealogy.
Perhaps you hail from a line of Tennessee
red clays? Or gleam with the frost-on-steel patina
of Mount St. Helens ash?
                              Never forget
you're here to bend beneath the thumb of faith.

Craft makes no excuses for the past:
put it behind you—neither claim it nor blame it.
We've all come through one firing or another.

Look—I've had enough. These nights, his voice
slams yours to the mat. Yours, the smaller
wrestler in the wrong weight class, lies there
so still, I count your pocks of silence
in fear they will add up to zero.

Last night I dreamed I slipped over you,
a second skin. You looked up startled
from brushing your teeth—and there we were,
joined tight in your mirror. Your wet fingers
traced my cheek, worn as the leather purse

that could hold all you need for leaving.
You were not repulsed. You knew power
when you touched it. We wasted no time
in fleeing but moved slow as a stone
shifts in water. Second thoughts caught up.

You tugged the shell of my nose from yours.
The holy pain of separation!
You peeled off my face. The rest of me
puddled at your feet. Something trifling
as the toothpaste tube needing its cap

called you back. These fresh cuttings of quince?
I'll plant a row of them between us.
He'll see thorns—call the hedge a spite fence.
I'll see early blooms and a leaf-wall
for barring the sounds of the hot months

with their windows open as fresh wounds.
Yes, enough! I want back what passes
for sleep. Help me plant quince between us.
You'll know the gaps where quail can slip through
and where they can shelter in their flight.

Sea life is rife with reversals. Oysters change
their sex as mating requires, and thus reflect
the androgyny of early God. Young males

among the California gray whales hump
each other. Bible-thumpers strain to square
this fact with how a whale mistook a sodden

Jonah for krill. Certain jellyfish grow
their tentacles two hundred feet in length
yet lack true eyes, brains, even hearts to pump

and steer their members' lust for food or love
on loitered nights when barkeeps yelp, "Last call."
Fifty folks could stand on a blue whale's tongue.

Why? To test if golf shoes tickle there?
An orca is a voluntary breather.
Half its brain must keep awake to work

the lungs—this lets the other half nod off.
Certain politicians tried this feat
back in '05, when *female* hurricanes

bitch-slapped the Gulf Coast states. Those caught asleep
dodged blame or aimed it. Even plankton lost
their innocence. For eons they massed as oil

to fuel our cars that stir the winds to *female*
Furies. Earth now warms fists that shake to
"shame on—blame on—anyone but me!"

A "blameless" search will score two million hits.
One blog ignores all layered guilt but this:
in the past thousand years, the sea and moon

each changed from *she* to *it*. This coincides
with science proving how the moon has inched
further from Earth each year. Tides are to blame.

his next words lost from the code
something not having settled
in the hot stomach pressing

its premise against my ribs
while coffee burns ciphers down
my throat and spinacheggmilk

spanakopita revolts
mild-mannered feta curdling
into this fallacy of

maldistributed middle
under cover of phyllo
something apologetic

as rice now gone rogue and
riddling caustic holes through my
logic and attentiveness

how to explain my forfeit
of his key words and gesture
how to bridge   gaps   in discourse

how to keep   his sudden pause
from souring   how to undo
the clabber-clot of phrases

how to decipher   the spill
of Pinot Gris   descanting
deep into the table's grain

Putting aside the grays found naturally
(as in dark lines along the spines of trout
above the complex stipples suggesting art),
we can differentiate between the pale
of dry curbs late in August and that dark

they turn once rain draws out their smells of clay
and limestone crushed before their time. And then
there's the gray a cloud-cap casts upon the hours
we call *gray days*, those times when a *gray mood*
keeps us from our sun-dependent plans.

And when street sewers clog during a flood,
we speak of *gray water*, both blockage and a sign
that we—it's all about us, after all—
can pass the blame for failing to press on,
the blame for thwarting us before our time.

1

Fay Fuller, dumpy as a sofa bolster
and the first female to scale Mount Rainier,
slept three nights in heavy skirts and bloomers.
She chose with care what she must lug and what
to leave behind. She drove long caulks and brads
through each boot's sole to nail her steps to ice.

2

Stieglitz's photograph of O'Keeffe's arm
against a car shows nails not stained with paint.
To that man behind the lens, these were not an artist's
hands. Fingers stroke a luxury of chrome.
Cold curves of fender. Wheel spoked nothing like
an open flower or female body part.

3

To render them more lifelike, Audubon
shot his models, spread their wings and nailed
them to wood, simulating flight. He killed
a sole white pelican to honor them
en masse? At church, sliding your nails between
crucified toes suggests the feet are webbed.

4

Nails show what to hold and what to lose.
They fight the ice that would slide you back.
A missing nail reveals how you failed to tack
with care. A horseshoe over the barn door
shifts upside down for want of a second nail.
Options leak from the dead gelding's shoe.

Persephone and Demeter in Ethiopia

Myth is instructed by history.
—Eavan Boland

The caption says it's spring along the banks
of the Ogaden. Spring and drought. The photo
shows us all along we've had it wrong:
the daughter coaxed her mother out of hell.

Not the other way around—see how
it's the old one who hangs back? How she fights
the girl's insistent tug on her shawl? See how
the mother's sandaled foot harrows the dust?

How the shadow planted by her toe takes root
to fix her there when all her muscles strain
to resist the pull of a daughter bent on change
and rain? This photograph forgives. Its female

objects, stark with beauty, come to us
in the dry spell before the dinner hour
to pardon ice cubes bickering over refills,
over who should shoulder this burden of thirst.

FROM

The Seven Deadlies

Interrobang Publications, 2013

On Learning from a Free Online Quiz
that You're a Facts Curator

This means you are highly intelligent and have picked up an impressive and unique collection of facts and figures over the years. You've got a remarkable vocabulary and exceptional math skills.
—from a follow-up email offering a 15-page report . . . for a substantial fee

Butter your butt and call you Biscuit—hot
from the oven, primed to soak up grease and praise!
Clever and fleet with figures, you divvy up
the offer: only six bucks and spare change

(per page) for more, more, more. You cuddle up
to the first deadly sin and wish the quiz
had let you flaunt more pet words: *wunjo, ilk,
rapscallion, sarasponda*—to name but four.

Proud and valued—is that too much to crave?
And who can prize us more than someone selling
selkie skins we slip inside to Braille,
with newfound fins, the vocabulary sea?

Some claim that in this quiz all *querents* find
their niches—their nests *fledged* with flattery?
A pox upon their house! May its numbers rot
off the street address! May pustules blight

their diction, *suppurate*, and leach it dry.
Sincerity? We'll take sweet talk, however
crudely slathered on. We'll savor its ooze
on our *digits*, tally up each lick and suck.

Once algae grows from her long hair, she's green,
subtle as moss, determined as a spore.

She's named for slæwð, the old, old word for slow,
and slow she is, hung from her bough of lunch.

A branch of cecropia: digestion
can reach from one new moon until the next.

Forget that Dante twined despair with sloth.
He never knew our plodding heroine.

Hung topsy-turvy from its branch, the vice
becomes the virtue of glad, deliberate care.

Get a hammock to sling you belly-up.
Lean back and slowly gnaw your green-shoot plans.

Bare your feet. Consider your extra toes
clutter from a life of wastrel haste.

Potluck

We are canapés for feasts that never start.
Angels-on-horseback, we shuck our shells,
spread our glutinous wings,
and wait for wolf,
gulp, swill.

Gluttons for *ahead*, we swap recipes
for hors d'oeuvres never made—forgetting
how few RSVPs
sought us out.
Pot-*luck*?

The satay sizzles on its bamboo stick,
our present skewered by its past.
The future rides on smoke:
a whiff of sear
and singe.

On the grill, scampi tighten into fists.
No one brought the main-course dish.
Forgotten in its pot,
its muscle—luck—
boils off.

after Baudelaire

See the viol? the knife, the fire, the poison?
The first one plays to the others' violence,
embroiders sound with artful and distracting
stitches, and so scorns ordinary life.

True, we turn to zoos of exotic beasts
for emblems of wild vices. Panther, wolf,
hyena, snake—behind their bars they teach
us to tell fear from shivering titillation.

This is where I bitch-slap you and call
you *hypocrite*—then hug you as my match,
my twin, and claim our common enemy
is the Great Yawn. Feeling confused, abused?

Once abstractions lose their teeth, we pimp
their former peril. Safe in shallow puddles
mucked by bad translation, we can fret
how the bawds who most fear ennui die of it.

At the Klamath River's mouth, sea lions wait.
The salmon end their shift from salt to fresh
in waters mingling both. They start upstream
to breed and die if they make it past seal-teeth
that take the belly only. Orcas scarce,
sea lions thrive on salmon and old laws.
To break those, Yuroks wear the skin of night.
Their rifles pledge more fish on the sun's return.

Ocean, land, and sky—we polish all
until we hold the mirror to show ourselves
reflected in the surge of sea, the urge
of fish, of seal. What to save? What to waste?
At dawn, where redwood logs both trace and ride
the tide, furred carcasses bob belly-up
above the newly gathered salmon school
awaiting change and risk at the Klamath's mouth.

On public television, in slow, slight strokes,
an old Jain sweeps his porch. He works to save
termites from the tread of looming guests.

If he's got it right, we could return as bugs
ravening for wood. Bamboo, oak, elm—
any flavor, as long as it is dead.

We'll chew a cud sodden with helpful microbes
and enzymes of the possible. We'll gnaw
to lift the gluttonous self to higher use.

Tunnel, excrete. A city of runnels mounds
in our wake. Symbiosis. Colony.
The tube that passes for the termite heart

requires we feed our fellows to meet this goal
we flunked in human form. We come on wings.
At the scent of wood, we shed them in a flick.

There's no turning back. New pulp, new purpose.
Without our human sense of geometry,
do we keep faith with the circle's elegance:

to the line returning to itself? If not,
we aim for this: to lose all sense of how
the old, old end will never change. Chew on.

"Lakes," say ladders, "are content to lay low—they lack the drive to rise to higher rungs!" According to the stepladder in the pantry, lakes are shiftless. Nothing moves them: wind scarcely ruffles a lake's skin of mirrors. Hence, "Vanity, thy name is lake!" the ladders exclaim. They tell us lakes are cowards, fools. They point out how a bully frog will harangue its pond (a would-be lake) all the moon long. "Our element— it's superior!" ladders claim. "Creatures of air, we frame it as we rise!"

As for the lakes,
their shoulders shrug a ripple in reply.
Loons are calling. Solitary lakes without a hope
of finding mates will play the servant's heart and help
night birds and frogs find theirs. Such longing stretches further
over water than wind can carry it, extends farther than a ladder
can ever reach. Ponds going dry in summer know this truth:
how wooden ladders sometimes slip off docks and learn
that air betrays. Sodden with loathed water, weighed
down beneath envy's feet, they lose all will
to float—and sink.

FROM

What Euclid's Third Axiom Neglects to Mention about Circles

White Pine Press, 2013

can give us our bearings where we're lost.
Things vast and physical point the way.
Take the earth's geology of scars:
from each new shape-shift we learn caution.

Trickier than plants or beasts, landforms
deceive, given the chance. Fumaroles,
domes, tuff, unloading and mass wasting:
any list conceals as it contains.

Distinguish what's essential from mere
clutter. Take two plains: the Snake River's
and the Serengeti's. See the tricks
of likeness? Plains vary more than ducks,

volcanic necks, far more than daisies.
We map terrain best once we've left it,
a new land mass already playing
the slut, promising clean slates and shales.

Never oversimplify causes.
True, three forces reshape our world's skin:
that first igneous creep of desire;
the slow, harsh dismantling of surface;

then rupture—one plane abandoning
the other over a fault or two.
In our study we will, of course, cite
slides, soil creeps, various erosions.

We will speak of what we cannot say.

The Hubble Space Telescope: A Story of Damage and Repair

Earlier, an astronaut ate fruit.
Strips of banana peel floated up
to hide the soft flesh.
A man and woman
enter the vast and airless garden.

The man seems less alive than the straps
and the tubes snaking
from the tool kit clamped
at his missing rib. Earlier still,
his empty spacesuit bobbed. Its fingers

groped slowly, with no
curiosity.
The couple floats to fix something small
as an apple core to this adrift
and knowing trunk—yet

which will be restored,
vision or blindness? The woman's slow
apologetic dance promises
whatever it takes
to make things right.

Today we'll see a few things out of place.
Those oranges, big as heads, are just for show
and taste like lint. In one day, their tree sucks
dry a saguaro's year. (We'll take the safe
route and handle this through travelogue.)

We'll drive south, out to the *Dove of the Desert*—out
to that wincing-white Mission of San Xavier.
For miles it falters over the hot road's
false water like a crippled dove. Its second
tower is domeless, clipped like a wing. At first
you dream it whole, then take comfort knowing
even Jesuits can fail. The one
who raised this mission sowed pale wheat that leached
color from maize. He brought in sheep and cattle
thirsty as those oranges. Call the missing
dome his penance for hauling here too much
of what he should have left behind.

                                    Be warned!—
the chapel shocks tourists with effigies
the colors of wild corn. The wooden saints
flaunt satin robes Papago women stitch
to hold the charms petitioners pin to cloth.
Silver pleas of hearts, arms, lungs, and legs:
each a prayer for parts that fail, for wounded
wings or domes. Outside, barbed ocotillo
climbs the Hill of the Holy Cross. On top,
a pair of bronze and shrapnel-maned lions squat
where pumas used to sun. From there we'll watch
the skies remember maize with colors so dead

and holy, any painter who steals such relics
draws the curse of sentimental to his brush.

Sunset will banner clouds with rose and gold
and balm scarred hills with purple spreading down
to the mission-dove at roost. Before the sun
goes limp as a yolk, we'll find the place to stand
to see it flame as it crowns the empty tower,
embers the stucco twin—until they match:
a dome of sun mirrored by its moon dome
it soon must leave behind. For one long breath,
this dove's healed wing will soar in borrowed grace
before the sun loses its hold, and falls.

First Breakfast Out after Parting

At the next table
an old couple, yet not one.
Questions they ask each other betray
a green history with shallow roots.

The terrible sounds
of forks and spoons making love
in quick trysts on scratched, thick porcelain.
Muffled shrieks of bussed, abandoned plates.

My grandmother keeps me posted
from Oregon. News clippings on potato
virtues come coupled in envelopes
with news of earthquakes or crib deaths,
as though potatoes hold the cure
if only puréed in time and force-fed
to all babies and the San Andreas Fault.

She's afraid I'll lose myself in this city
and not make it back to garden next spring.
What we call a potato's eyes are feelers,
rippling probes of a mole's nose
nudging past soil to the salvation of light.
Perhaps she trusts potatoes
to tunnel my way out of any darkness.

This is winter's longest night.
Today in a Bloomsbury greengrocer's,
I bought a potato smelling of the earth's armpit
where it can incubate like the fabled prisoner's egg
that hatched a chick and the warden's goodwill.
Tonight I heap my desk with clippings from *The Oregonian*,
eggs, potatoes, and other humble forms of prayer.

The potato smells of harrowing,
of distressing the soil in the faith
such pain will bring release.
In the silence of my grandmother's cellar,
flats of seed potatoes pray for spring and revival.
Outside, this city hums like homing bees.
I heft my potato, ticket for the passage back.

we lose our history. Last night I lost Poros.
We were walking miles back to our budget villa.
At first the road stretched long and whole before us.
For a moment more I could still name for you
the open-air taverna just ahead
and the military school where boys rehearse
for the day their navy drills will really count.

I could still make out the cemetery gates
where we watched the widow enter with a priest
to claim the bones from last year's burial
in preparation for this year's internment,
blessed with wine, the one that really matters.

I could still make out the steep ascent and curve
of the road we took on battered, rented Vespas,
sputtering up to Poseidon's temple ruins
where Demosthenes fled, eluding capture
long enough to choose poison instead.

One instant more the path ahead was whole—
then my panic to rush before the island
disappeared, image by image, patch by patch,
before our villa vanished, carrying off
its balcony where we drank retsina,
its rows of roses in caked dirt, its dock
rocking all night like a toy wooden mouse
battered by seas domestic as cats.

Scene by scene I relinquish our history,
dissolved in the acid hiss of deceit. I lose
places we meant to revisit once we got
something right—like learning the local tongue.
How terrible is this suspicion
the rehearsal is the only event.

*   *   *

A few years before my grandmother died,
she announced *The Great Uncluttering.*
My task was to empty the Cousins' Trunk.
I expected the torn, faded costumes,
the hand puppets with musty rubber heads—
but not all those score pads to games long lost,
their broken pieces now turning up
in the archeological digs of the new
towheaded generation squatting
in the backyard, our former holding.
Those score sheets? We played their games to bits,
yet saved the pads for when we *really* played.
Who taught us this—to hunker on the fringe
of a future that never quite arrives?

*   *   *

Yesterday a woman I've never met
told me on the phone about her struggle
to keep her son from killing himself.
She needed her rabbi, but he was tied up.
"Why," she asked, "am I telling this, to you,

a stranger?" "You are telling me," I said,
because I *am* a stranger." *And because,*
I told myself, *I'm her board game's scratch paper.*

Act now, or nothing matters until too late,
until events you did not practice for
wring dry the calendar of days deferred.
Even if you learn the local tongue,
it's now too late for Poros, for places where
the heart can't bear to sputter its worn-out
Vespa up steep hills to temple ruins.

Do you notice how we time it to reach the booth
as it shuts down? How it takes the day's *last* tickets
to throb with power to jump-start the pulse?
Dogged as compass needles seeking north,
we zag past javelinas, snakes, and wolves
to tunnel down where beavers swim and gawk
through underwater windows of *our* cage.

Yet it's the other tank that draws us in—
its otters paying us no heed. They slice
their water, sure as knives at cutting ties.
Pressed on glass as cool as seraphs' wings,
we seem to slough the cluttered self
and swim beside them, fleet in borrowed grace.

In such necessary fiction, we can lose
ourselves, though not for long. We've timed it close:
the bell soon shrills to start the keeper's rounds.
Before we idle too loose, he shoos us up
the concrete ramp as the pen of crippled hawks
scolds the dusk. Climb swiftly and the gut
twinges as it does when elevators
lug us into paltry reckonings
with gravity.
                        What else do we ever risk?
What besides this warning of the engine's
frailty? How it will slip its hold and fall,
slow as a nail sinks in spent motor oil.

Instructions for Fall Cleaning

Those cracked and hateful plates—now throw them out,
out with the cousin no one loves, the one
who gave your mother that last cough though begged
to keep all fever away. Out as well
with the man who shrank from deaths startling you home
to steel-framed rented beds, rails up or down
as the hour's task required. Cast out the stack
of condolence cards you meant to answer then,
their rubber bands now sagging with regret.

Fall trains us how to clean muddles, how trees
find themselves in baring, how sloughing lifts
like wings, refines whoever toils at cleaning.
October is for sorting books and words:
rogue Volume Twos mis-shelved far from their Ones,
forget misplaced before *forgive*. Though once
you can forget for weeks—months—at a time,
forgiveness comes cheap, at no expense of pride.

Fall's for tackling clutter. June rehearsed
you for this task. When you deadhead a rose,
you make your cut above a five-leafed twig
and trust this paradox: prune to increase.
In fall we learn no matter how cold it turns,
truth is what you tuck, tidy, restored,
back in the drawer emptied of broken bits
clacking for glue. Handles bereft of cups,
a pair of rings no fingers will reclaim.
The photos torn, the missing face revoked.

On to the boxes stacked along the car.
Into the dumpster with them—open none.
Surely the damp has wrecked the trays of slides,
the red-rimmed film curled loose in cardboard cells.
The Shetland Islands—free them frame by frame.
Release the puffins, gannets, razorbills.
Let them fly to burrows, rocky nests.
The birds of Kiribati, release them next.
Back to the atoll's bonefish flats with them.
The booby first. Throat scarlet with desire,
he hovered over your fly rod, a twig
denied his nest. The Christmas Island wren.
Save her for last, then let her go as well.

I will leave behind the foothills of the peak
I never meant to climb. The further I trek,

the more all fractured sounds will join as strokes
of keels that harrow water, sending forth

waves to flood all trace of my spent shore
in a rhythm of *assault, retreat, retrench,*

escape. When poised between the land and sea,
first we must lose lupine. Let lapse its name.

Next, names for columbine, dog violet,
translucent Indian pipe—waxy, pale,

feeding on leaf-decay. Relinquish what
isolates part from whole: *panicle, bract,*

stigma. Keep watch for what we once called *flowers.*
One, blood-bright, shaped like a bottle-brush,

will serve as sign to scour, then melt, then merge
into the blur of bouquet. This fluid state

is what we seek for growing the gills and verve
to swim from landlocked memory and need.

These hours, ambivalent as fog
swagging porch cobwebs with wet beads.
The blurred beyond? Confused gray cells.
Time's spine slow-broken on the rack.

"Algebra" means to set cracked bones,
faith that numbers work to heal.
Open the door onto the yard.
Let its threshold and header serve

as equal sign. Through the cataracts
of mist beyond, red tulips nod
over their homework, managing
to multiply despite distractions.

Trace the fracture line that links
you through the copula door to bright
tulips: clear proof you factor in
future equations for repair.

Salvation by Botany

Twice last night I dreamed the house burned down.
In the first dream, I couldn't think of what to save.
Panic-wired, I fled, flames at my back.
Daphne-like, I turned into a bush
flocked with fire-retardant, alarmed yet safe.

The second dream, I packed—sensibly packed—
a satchel crammed with underwear and books
for those long days it takes our life's lost bags
to find us after flight. This time flames licked
from a space heater I've never seen before.

It budded off one end of its taut, black cord,
unfurled hibiscus petals veined with fire.
Above its plug that suckled at the wall,
the outlet's unused nostrils snorted smoke
(dreams sort out such strange anatomy).

This time, I grabbed my *Basic Wiring* book,
published by the aptly named Time-Life,
that pesky pair dreams muddle, yet refine.
I looked up "circuitry." Diagramed wires
curled into vines of uncanny botany.

I should have found the circuit-breaker box,
tripped the main, then hosed the fire out.
Instead, I woke to dark. And to garden plans
for coaxing fireweed into thyme's tame bed.
Fireweed? Charred soil's savior. Forward, wild.

Basic Training

During a ceasefire
in our war games
my cousin proves

you can kill a slug
with something slight
as the tight bud

of a dandelion
on its hollow
stalk. We're ten, eight.

Whap-whap! How tender
the flesh, how it
opens like trust.

Balancing the Checkbook during US Air Strikes

Outside my window, the flak
of rain swags a ravaged web.
The spider, a refugee
from the recent cloudburst,
starts her repairs in the lull

between downpours and updates
on the radio. Beyond:
the slow strafe of fog
along Ole Hanson Creek
and regiments of redwoods.

Here, at the Pacific's edge,
it's dusk. There, it's dawn
bringing a loud rain of bombs.
I open the Jøtul stove,
load its chamber with madrone.

Maroon curls of bark
parachute to the hearth bricks
postponing their reckoning
with flame. In the dimming light,
numbers from the bank

seize their chance to open fire.
The solar calculator
flutters a surrender code.
I face the window.
My reflection on the pane

frames the spider balancing
on her threads. Across her spreads
a fog of woman
in a ceasefire of numbers,
caught fast in strands of war.

Grandmother, I am the warden shadow
vigilant across your sheets
when they hiss like waves drawn flat.

I thought I heard you call me
from sofa lumps to your side.
A distant dog scolded the moon.

At dinner when you looked ahead
to your birthday this fall,
you stopped dead on the thought

today was *your* grandmother's
one hundred and sixtieth.
How could anyone die so long?

We would not let the silence win.
We made you embroider her in air,
cross-stitch her *norsk* way with potatoes.

Like smoke from a green-wood fire,
the sepia woman left the album
to hover your oil-clothed table.

We are selfish ears. Your voice
is the thread seaming cousin to cousin.
We hound your sleep. We keep you

patching the quilt you would rest beneath.
To catch the stitches you drop at night,
I am the warden shadow across your sheets.

She's trapped. She dangles from a walnut branch,
laced fingers knuckle-locked and losing feeling.
Through the window trading flaccid winter air
for May's first heat hefting its floral scents
drift sounds of dentures clacking disapproval
of the bride's choice of processional music.
It's to come from Brahms' *First* rather than the tune

Here comes the bride, her little cousins hum
as they goosestep Ken and Barbie yet again
to the Nike-shoebox altar swagged with sprigs
of wilting lilac smelling nothing like
lilac sachets in Aunt Pearl's girdle drawer.
She will not cry for help from voices scoffing,
"No resolution!" "Awkwardly fades off."

Where her numb hands end and the tree begins, she feels
nothing like herself yet on the verge . . . of what?
A wild kick off the trunk. One gangly leg
up and over the shackle-branch. She's free.
Her scrape? Her secret—saved from cheeks afire.
Later, the needle plunked to vinyl, minute four,
she hears what made the women *huff* and *tsk*:

a yearning unfulfilled despite the music
tiptoeing after . . . what? Steps nothing like
Barbie's curtailed feet rigidly arched
for plastic slippers scattered in the grass.
From its coiled calling, the needle seeks release
as music climbs its trunk of notes, hangs there,
transforms to stringed and lingering sighs of longing,

like fingers locked around a branch and losing
all sense of self. They tingle yet. She runs
to the daphne, strips its end-of-season blooms,
rolls in them like a pup, paws and claws
their tang until the quivers of strange fire
leave her hands. Her pulse returns, renewed.
Drumming out new music. Nothing like.

In November, Shades of Blue

When his brown eyes turned back to blue
we knew his death was days away
yet stalled the engine's need to start
those final things it had to say.

We spoke about anything else—
the vase of flowers with the ugly name
of *Scabiosa* near his bed.
Couldn't their lavender-blue claim

a better nickname than the "Scabs"
he called them? There, in his garden book,
we found their folk-name, *Mourning Bride*,
proving no matter where you look

to find escape, you circle back
to where you started in the heart,
that stubborn motor where the words
strain to turn over before they start.

By then his eyes had turned the shade
all newborns share: a blue so clear
no flower can ever get it right.
That circling back felt enough to cheer

his final week when skies refused
to show their blue. Over our train
of headlights, clumps of gray clouds bloomed
like dingy peonies the rain

will batter clean. Among the wreaths,
we idled, cars with open hoods
awaiting closing. A lone crow
circled the dim and far-off woods.

Lessons from the Ghost House on Walnut Street
Once Widening the Road Felled Those Namesake Trees

Smell, the first lesson, came from emptied halves
of lemons near the splashboard of the sink
wide enough to bathe a fractious toddler.
The grown-up crowded fingers in a cup
of lemon rind, digging to force damp pulp
beneath the nails, a task performed each dusk
of the farming day with its attendant dirt.
In this fingertip confessional, all stains
but those from the green husks of now-gone walnuts
faded as cuts and punctures stung alert
and granted absolution from infection.
Useful: this homily on how hurt can cleanse
and keep us safe from larger, future grief.

The final lesson came the day the clan
watched the bulldozer take the last wall down:
that stubborn west side where the old folks died
twenty years apart and both in peace.
Gone, that narrow strip between close doorframes
smeared with penciled names, dates, and the marks
for annual heights of children shooting past
their grandmother, the only one allowed
shoes for the smudge that lied she stretched five feet.
The lesson from the rubbled walls goes thus:
measurements are made to be lost at length,
as are stains, Walnut's walnuts—all memories
but the odd few linked by their scents to pain.

The day my mother died, I learned a secret
kept wherever we tend to tuck such things:
in the skull or in that muscle our ribs protect.

Before I tell you, let me use a white
crayon on white paper to draw for you
my mother's last kitchen. You'll have to slant

my sketch to light to find the room in all
that white, concealing wax. The four black spirals
depict the heating coils of her spotless (white)

electric range. They curve nothing like the inner
whorls of the nautilus shell whose golden numbers
count down until they reach that final room,

polished and still, the pulse and muscle gone.
Her white, immaculate kitchen deep inside
her small, white-shingled house. The dread of friends

shamed by how she kept out dirt and dust,
those small ideas for the care the world requires.
At dusk, our deathwatch done, my father and I

come to the white, white kitchen. I fill *three* mugs.
We sit in silence, far too tired for grief
or coffee, both gone stale. All of a sudden

my father wants to know have I ever wondered
why I had no brothers? sisters? In truth,
in my cousin-cluttered childhood, I never had.

School nights and summers we smudged and grimed
our grandma's butter-colored kitchen spread
open like one of her tattered storybooks.

So here's my mother's secret I promised you.
At my birth—alone, when he was off to war—
yes, at my birth my mother heard *blue* voices.

Over and over he read her letter's cursive terror:
what if their children bore this tint of madness?
They must not risk any more. I spoon all this

into my coffee, there in the white, white kitchen
allowed at last to press dust to its breast.
Minutes streak down the wan face of the clock.

Mother, if you can hear me—please know this:
I trust in voices. I'll take them any color.
Had I known your burden, we might have laughed

in your white kitchen while our coffee mugs
drew their wet rings on your bright, spotless counters.
When you felt the need at last, you could wipe away

those clear brown drafts of far, possible planets,
some whole, some not. Their borders closed—or open
and undecided as our years ahead.

"One thing about those Olson women: hard-workers, year in and out."
—overheard at the Scholls Grange Annual Chuckwagon and Craft Bazaar

Olson women worship planting and sausage.
We stuff seeds in casings of moist, spring soil.

In summer, we mothers of gorgeous sweat
water, weed, and hoe all the hot sky long.

We knead allspice, pepper, into raw, chopped meat.
Talk healing. Smear peach pulp on winter aches.

As we heap food on work's altar each fall,
vine maples slough scarlet leaves at our feet.

It comes to this: a camellia leaf lies
long on the ground in a fellowship of duff.
Larvae strip the leaf to an elegant theory
of itself. The bared veins, finer than wasp
antennae, cast their desiccated net
to the edge of their known world. Angels cease
dancing on heads of pins and forsake their census
to marvel at this tracery decay.

Likewise, the family house must cast off doors.
Drawers must pull out, flip over, and shed their hoards:
the tarnished baby spoon and sugar tongs,
half-used candles, lids to long-gone jars,
and schemes for leaf-miners to carry off
what never should be saved. When life is clutter,
the goal is rapture. The means? Ravish, devour.
All that remains will let through light at last.

FROM

The Last Night of Maskmaking

Unpublished

The Selkie Discovers the Information Age

As I looked the other way, he took my skin.
He must have seen me surface from the hiss
of seafoam, watched me roll and lurch ashore,
heard the suck as I slid from pelt to sand.

I felt my fin-flesh split as fingers, toes.
The other changes came quick upon the heels,
the legs, arms, and breasts. Surely my eyes
remain the same? At the faint crunch of shells

I turned and saw him vanish round a dune.
That's the instant I became a woman
stuck on land. He'll come to claim me once
he hides my pelt. Those are the old, old rules.

Our ancient tales warn of such beachings—warn
these flailing limbs can't swim me home again.
I'm to make peace with them and search his haunts
to reclaim the fur-gate to my stronger self.

That much I knew. Yet no one warned the mind
could change as well—or how each moment adds
its load of land-facts, details like how things work,
what they're named. See? Just like that I know

actuary tables and can explain
holograms and how their manganese
particles flit and reshape as delicate
artifice. So much information!—

so little knowledge. And how's my hermit crab
mind to fit all this clutter in its shell?
Must I discard, forget, how limpets grip
their rocks? How fanned kelp flirts with fins? Just now

something important about coral reefs
floated away. My selkie sense of future
dims. That image winking out—it's me
tidying up his house, my head a-slosh

with recipes for fishcakes, stew. My eyes
have shrunk and leached from black to gray. I move
our bed and knock a floor plank loose. Concealed
below I find a stiff and stinking hide.

I drag it off to the burn-pile outside.

I find here that before men filched
what they named *alphabet*,
letters called themselves
matrika: mothers.

Mothers of words,
invented by Vac,
Mother of Creation,
the goddess Voice.

This is not about women
versus men. This is
about tampering, forgetting,
as in "my mother

tampered with my father's
law school papers"
versus "my mother—
and everyone else—

forgot she wrote
my father's papers."
Alas, the unfortunate sex
of respective parents

muddles the issue
of Vac wanting her due.
Alien gods require space
but not much worship.

Every painted god, its niche;
every Toyota, its garage.
Vac understands our age
and asks only for her voice back,

for the space of three *matrika*
in which to hole up. In return—
and what god worth its paint job
doesn't give us something

for our money?—she promises
to tidy up those combustible piles
of dusty, collapsed letters.
She would sort them into

words to recycle,
words to forget, words
she never meant to leave us.
Words as opposed as *war*

and *free* she would untangle
from *zone* and sort like socks
hot and snapping from the dryer.
She would deliver us

from clutter, from static.
I could use such extra help.
This is the value of old gods:
their cost-effective and easy

comfort. I would stoop
even lower to catch another
slipping from the dry page
of an otherwise useless book.

Career Day at Union High: The Bryologist Speaks of Working with Mosses

Mosses are masters of time,
its management. They teach us
to thrive outside it.

First, discover the secret
separating your higher
from your lower plants.

The former produce seeds.
So much infringes
on their capacity to live.

Spores of the vernacular
are not as insistent
and need so little sun.

There are those who will tell you
mosses and North Americans
have no true roots.

Yet even liverworts
have been observed lying
prostrate on ancestral graves.

Others will argue the vulgar
are winning through numbers.
True, but at what cost?

Consider the loss column
for each curve of a fiddlehead:
no pain, *some* gain.

Ferns are not my business,
yet fossils tell us of those
who chose to give up seeds

so the vulnerable stages
of early growth could be
bypassed with little risk.

Never underestimate
the danger of imagination—
other seeds.

Vascular systems?
Highly overrated, you'll find.
I could go on and on

about direct absorption,
its instant gratification,
simplicity.

Job security
and room to branch out?
You can anchor yourself with rhizoids!

Everything is before you
within reach—there!—
in the moist, necessary air.

The Estranged Mother Writes to Acknowledge
Her Daughter's Gift

Thank you for the startling wall hanging.
It matches the poinsettia
no one thought to give me.

It's cold here. Robins slouch on fences,
marking time and fence posts with lime.
We all do what we must.

Three black-caps chitter their victory.
The earth inherited at last,
why bother with meekness?

Chickadees have a gift for winter,
for denying it while springing
glibly from twig to twig.

Unlike the robin, they seem not here.
They are off in their own season
of heedless somersaults.

Each day fewer holly berries hang
as red charms against these black boughs.
And then, such shriveling.

These short, gray days of switching perches
to dodge wind. This indecision.
What's a robin to do?

Wait for accidental sacrifice
of surfacing worms? Is it time
to break the birdbath's ice?

Outside this window, you used to lie
on the first snow, your arms sculpting
the quick wings of angels.

Snow blurs the fissures in sullen ground,
forgives the year's bare spots and ruts,
which brings me back to birds.

Say a robin's grudges are balanced
by her faculty to admire
the younger, cheeky bird.

How to overcome a history
full of territorial rifts?
I flip through the field guide.

Can robin find the notes to explain?
Won't her *put-put-put* be misread
as shrill imperatives?

Pages separate the two. Their calls
are spelled out in frail italics.
There must be common ground.

Daughter, you've always been so clever
at translation. All calls are cries
for something, if only

we could read them right.

The Fairy Godmother's Rebuke on the Coach Ride Home

You say your slippers nip and cram your toes?
Your clammy silks hug tight your flesh, like scum
on early autumn ponds? Your sequins bite
your neck, then flake away like dandruff duff
on those widowed shoulders at the ball? You fear
the poet's wrong—your veggie love won't grow
as promised ("vaster than empires and more slow").

Enough with whining! Gussied up for myth
and storied fame? I warned you of this crush
and squeeze. Squash happens, girl! It's pumpkin time.

Complaint of the Double-Sided Comb from Sweden

They call this place the Junk Drawer. Not my first
retirement home for gimcrack. Here I dwell

with broken bits of toys outgrown, a clutch
of rubber bands gone slack with age, the stubs

of candles hoarded—god-knows-why—and lids
widowed from jars. Essential once, I led

a double life. No longer than his thumb,
I smoothed my voyager's scalp and beard, then turned

my finer, better half to seek out nits.
A century in drawers proved time forgets

you once your mission ends. This afternoon
a small boy rummaged through this space

and asked my use. He sniggered when they shrunk
me to the single word of *comb*. Had I

a mouth around these teeth, I could have screamed,
"and made of brass, declined as *brassy, brazen*—

so beware my bite, you little *skithuvud*!"
Any lapsed god out there? Loki, perhaps?

Smite such ignorance with the curse of lice!
Restore my sense of purpose—and your own.

In Praise of Me, Vinegar

Think of me as wine with an attitude,
bred in a bitter neighborhood, the kind
you drive through fast, doors locked and windows up,
tires on the watch for ice picks, broken glass.
Over time, they say I go sour, bad.

Yet I'm primed to do your dirty work. I'll scour
those greasy squatters from dank banks of sinks.
(Voyeur! You like to watch me rough them up.)
A TV chef hires hit-man vinegar
to beat the starch out of spring's first strawberries.

You know the type: the fruit that loiters round
the bowl. All flirt. No sign of sweet surrender.
First the chef cuts such berries down to size.
then gets me—bad-boy vinegar—to work
them over till they go limp with loss of what

they meant to hold back for another month.
Can you smell their red welts weeping *sugar, sugar*?
Cider, balsamic, or one of the wine gang—
take a deep whiff, a cleansing suck. Just don't
ask us to pickle what you should toss out:

orange peel, watermelon rind, memories.
You've soaked in suffering long enough. It's time
to end your season of sloughing, loss. Trash. Toss.
So call on me, your hoodlum, vinegar.
I'll clean your counters, windows, floors, and clock.

The Coach Ride Back

Through glass my feet show bruised and pinched,
my toes can't shift or feel.
Like honey crammed in clammy cells,
my joy should overflow.

That must be what the sisters thought
as we danced past their chairs.
I sensed it in their glacial squints
fixed on my crystal steps.

Before tonight, without a glance,
he passed my beauty by.
Then hours ago he fell in love
with coif and gown a-bling.

Consider the alternative,
m'dear (I tell my soul).
Choose dull-and-ash or dull-and-gilt,
small comfort lies in one.

The ash? more cinders, snubs, and toil,
though honest is that path.
The gilt? a life of ease and fame
where guise and gossip reign.

Time is bearing down on me,
my fate is pressing close.
Rose petals crushed on silken seats,
but all I smell is squash.

The Latex Half-Mask Addresses the Mask Maker

Now that you've pried me from my plaster mold
and find me weak and pliant, you'll stretch and pinch
my skin before it hardens. That much I know.
While my rubber-stink of curiosity
lingers, humor me and share your plans.
Am I to stay ageless, androgynous?
And why no mouth beneath this beaklike nose?
That space reserved for shapeshifters to breed
voices? The man whose avatar prowls online
for love—scrap scorn and slip me over him.
The muted teen who cuts herself in secret?
Before you weave her words to speak through me,
slide beneath her skin of scars and feel
what carves her deeper than her razor's kiss.
Pile up their details, maker. I'll lend them voice
and do my part to stave off shrinkage, loss.
That's my offer. The listening's left to you.

What the Apple Whispered

". . . but Eve—Eve just wanted to know shit."
—Hedwig and the Angry Inch

Knowledge is Trickster. Swallow if you will.
It makes no difference now—the bite was all.
Look down. Give nothing away. We are observed
and have little time. Yes, I'm the speech from where

sweet-tartness meets your tongue, yet I'm not *your* words.
Never mind the wonder of it—this
is what you bargained for: burden, truth.
Take a last look around you. Poverty

of imagination always stripped this place.
Only now can you see its nakedness.
Joy and pain—daughters and sons—will follow you.
Those who wield the intellect's weakest knives

will whittle God down to a trifling size
to suit them: god in their own image. Life—
as you are soon to learn—is full of such
reversals. Split to one gender and stripped

of power, God will lose credit for pulse
in far-off gardens, lose the knack to craft
new beasts from old drafts. See how your serpent-guide's
legs begin to wither? Some will call this

Punishment. Others will name it *Sauropod.*
Future tongues will curse you for this taste
of knowledge. Future men will chastise you
by denying souls to your daughters for a time.

No matter what you're called—Pandora, Eve,
Cassandra—you will never gain the trust
of fools. We're done. We've cleared the bowels of truth.
You will forget the wisdom my tree has shared—

except for this: compassion. Practice now—
stroke the lean beast hissing loss at your feet.
And before the flaming sword named *Forget* can hack
the gate to bits, lick my juice at your lips.

Nothing will taste this powerful again.

Excerpt from The Encyclopedia of Crises:
How To Identify a Mail Bomb

Check for leaks. Sniff oily stains.
       Bad signs.
Do muscles at the corners
       of your mouth
tic in time to something
       "metronome"?
Does the package quiver
       at your touch?
Or feel slimy as the bottom
       of a summer pond?
Is the postal carrier
       unfamiliar? sly?
Or like the parcel: sporting
       protrusions? dents?

       Alone at home
and in your chambered heart
       dial 9-1-1.
Be patient. This is what
       you live for:
waiting for someone
not you.

How to Housebreak a Shadow

After catastrophe, subside in silk
beneath harsh lights and over the day's fresh
newspapers spread across the floor.

During this convalescent sprawl, console
the shadow sniffing, cowering, at your feet.
Pat it and point the papers out.

Tell it the intricate, shadow-free frost etched
on your pane is winter's fleeting jealousy.
Coax and hoist its confidence.

Push its nose in each failure—yet grant
it stints of bliss and frolic, at the end
of the mindful leash that scolds restraint.

Once it shows (fractured and ambivalent)
collared obedience, reward it. Call it
Grief and feed it beneath your sink.

The Toadstool Blames His Victim

How the abuser thinks—understanding this can alert me to call up my exit strategies.
—from a journaling project for a women's shelter

You strayed here. Why? To dream chanterelles?
No one beckoned you to these fogged trees,
leaves weighted down in slick, wet sleep. Tell me—
was it my danger? The dank flirt of it?
You should have stuck with mushrooms—those dull louts
plumped in sterile dung for mini-marts.
You know I never meant to hurt your liver.
You stalked me and brought this on yourself.
You never looked deep within my soil.
There, I am vaster than you credit me.
Don't deny this: you scorn my family,
our fungi doom—how again, again, we're forced
to shove our way up to your meager light.

Mechanics shake their heads. My cylinders
misfire. My carburetor flubs the mix
of fuel with air, and gaskets wheeze replace.
Sentiment's sediments have sludged my points.
In its pig-iron gut, the engine grunts and stalls.
Delphi Auto tallies my dents and loss,
deducts them from this oracle-estimate
of my worth, the crew chanting depreciation.
Day by day my market value sinks.
What is left to broker? Trade-in roadways
for footpath, bike lane, bus? When the last-chance
mechanic turns his back, I roll all windows
down. I leave the doors ajar, unlocked.
I leave the key in the ignition. I leave.

The Last Night of Maskmaking

for Carolyn Lehman

I took on the face and ways of a new person
walked in him and was redeemed
—Ode 17, *The Odes of Solomon*, a Gnostic text

We bring dates, hummus, stuffed tomatoes, bread
exhaling warm yeast. Nothing made from meat.
After dinner, we feast again on color:
cerulean blue, burnt umber, acra red.
Six women mix more acrylics than needed
unless we paint our bodies to match our masks.
No one here chose to work in leather—all
stuck with and to papier-mâché's weak flesh,
layer by layer its strength built up.

Our only men who show for this last class
are the two masks our pair of lovers paint:
a blue rain god, his lips pursed to blow storms,
and the fisher king, wistful about his eyes.
Both males are comic, frail as paper bits
before their bracing baptism in glue.

Tonight, our mother and daughter—who scarcely spoke
to one another all term—paint their ghouls
more human each brushstroke. Our ER nurse
fledges her raven's head while my bird-beaked crone
grows age lines, forked like lightning, from her eyes.
Now and then we trade masks, pass them on
like communion cups, lift each and breathe through damp
nose holes, the fresh paint smelling a bit like blood.

The Latin word for mask is *persona*—not
a face to hide beneath. We slip the Self
when its engine stalls—or when we finally sense
the Other. Time to listen rather than
to cosset close the gang confessional
of I, *me, mine*. The rigid mouths of masks
release those voices we feel or steal. I slide
behind the fisher king and sigh for trout.

In a Gnostic text, the goddess Voice declares
she is the *mother of invention*, then
vanishes down a hole in the brittle scroll.

Tonight our teacher trades her masks for music.
Knot by knot, she drapes dried gourds in loose
jackets of beads. When she shakes this shekere,
glass whisks its rounded belly, conceiving sound.
Into the aged VCR, she slips
the video of her trip to Bali. Dim shapes
pulse on the screen to flutes and gongs and *thwungs*
from something like a wooden marimba tipped
on its side. We float on cymbals to the temple.
Masked dancers shake their shoulders as they chant
chak, chak, chak! coaxing Sanghyang into her trance
so she may learn what gods expect of us.

In Bali, maskmakers lead local priests
into the forest. The holy men must find
the trees where trapped faces await their carving.
Tonight, across the sea, six women sense
something caught inside, calling for release.

At home, unfinished masks await us all:
a toadstool, merfolk, the seven deadly sins.
None chosen for this final night—yet each
a prayer for all that fails us. All we fail.

Late in August, plans for Halloween
drew us here. Midway through October rains,
all talk of costume parties rinsed away.
Something never sought has found and named us
mothers of invention. With each new mask,
we shed more cluttered self.

                                We'll scatter back
to scattered lives. Yet this—this smelling meat
we didn't know we hungered for—this may
endure. This call to the servant's heart to join
both the priest and carver-guide to redeem

the forest of invention,
where live faces wait in trees.

FROM

Why I Won't Take My Jane Austen Action Figure Out of Her Packaging

Unpublished

For instance, here—in etching and collagraph—
a nocturnal scene we crave yet seldom see.
This tree lacks obvious roots and thus absolves
itself from all responsibility
for drawing water from the nearby lake
serene enough to chart the dithered path
of an off-stage moon. The stucco house affirms
this moon, its lakeward wall awash in light
launched from a point of faith beyond the frame.

We sense the etching's parenthetical
to our desire to know the moon exists
beyond our view—as do all absent fowl:
goatsuckers, frogmouths, oilbirds. For their sake
the imagination freckles the fancied moon's
wan face with pointillist specks to stand for gnats
whose whine of "take me now!" such birds oblige.

How quick the mind is to clutter when it needs
to purge the glut of detail. If this lake
is not responsible for the thirst of trees,
who themselves refuse to form a plan for roots,
surely we're freed from guilt for appetites
of birds who wait unbidden in the wings
to indulge the hankering imagination?
We yield from hunger to temptations art
permits us. This is your cautionary tale.

From the Lecture: "At the Roots of New World Art:
The Lithographs of John James Audubon"

Keep in mind, he always worked from death.
He roamed the woods, rifle in lieu of pen,
and shot his birds, then nailed, wired them in place.

Mammals proved more troublesome. The wounds—
entry and exit—from a single blast
might halve a meadow mouse. Still-death prevailed

where still-life once sufficed. The next slide, please:
Audubon's *American Red Fox.*
Note the steel trap. A Newhouse 2 or 3.

No other of his lithos sports it—though
in anxious times, he hawked all he could paint
in oils of otters poised in this steel embrace.

Our artist's hallmark? This rigor mortis grin:
mouth wide, teeth bared. Even his prairie dogs
and gophers flaunt incisors, smirk this way.

Some say this artist was in fact the son,
once dementia snared the father's mind.
Which would perhaps explain the modest sums

this picture brings at auction, that backwoods tent
pitched each open season on craft and art.
Back to our litho's chief detail and ruse—

this is how you prime a Newhouse trap:
pull the jaws apart, full-smirk. Prime the dog
and thumb it down. Then raise the pan. Next slide.

Yes to worm, mole, all burrowers who nudge,
snuffle, and ruck what surface-dwellers miss.
Yes to magpie, packrat, and all who seek
gewgaw and gimcrack. Yes to coyote, shrimp,
krill, and all scavengers who sense that salvage
suckers off salvation's root and who sieve
or sniff-and-paw what others snub as waste.

Yet no to swine and those content to wallow
and grunt in muck of their own making—nor
shall cows hold sway, nor other ruminants
partaking of redundant cuds. But yes
to genera both fish and fowl and all
half-humans (centaurs and merfolk,
to name but two). And yes to androgynies.

Likewise, yes to necessary fictions—
phoenix, griffon, cockatrice—although
the sorely used unicorn shall decline
and take his rest from shop-worn celebrity.
And no to sea anemones and others
who never change their stance—except the oyster,
coaxer of grit into luster of great worth.

No to prides and coveys, gaggles, flocks,
and their ilk—herds among whom none stands solely
forth. A beast of burden—donkey, camel,
elephant—shall only serve if paired
with a slight creature of no apparent use.
Perhaps the sugar glider? Smidgeon possum
who spreads her skin and sails on air for bliss.

Only this time, he dons a servile mob-cap
and gender-bends as Marilyn Monroe.
Her skin as pale as parsnips, she holds a plate
of bananas high above a table lost
in woods where she has also lost her way.
She finds herself a server for the three
artsy women sitting before a froth
of tatted lace. There's Picasso's wench in stripes,
a cubist teapot sprouting from her hand.

Nipples on her dirigible breasts aim up,
threatening to dispense cream—her two
companions hold their teacups out of range:
Mona Lisa and Modigliani's miss,
her neck as long as Marilyn's phallic fruit.
Three working women sitting down to tea,
taking a break from stints as beauty's objects—
all but mad Marilyn, now reduced to serving
other knock-off knock-outs made by men.

Perhaps she feels she's found her personal hell
and laments, *Celebrity, celebrity—*
wherefore art thou? while pouring into cups
bereft of saucers. Tea cakes scuttle off
their plates like roaches frantic for the dark.
To her dismay, her tray's one banana short
should the invitation come to take a seat
with these immortals. Yes, a banana missing,
and on the verge of consumption, every one.

Reading Milton in the Produce Department

I cannot praise a fugitive and cloistered virtue, unexercised and
unbreathed, that never sallies out and sees her adversary, but
slinks out of the race . . .
—Areopagitica

In this safe garden, no lizard flicks
from bunched spinach to covet tomatoes
we press and heft.

Here, no winter-withered apple
waits to snigger at our fatal touch.
All fruit is baptized

in oil against a second fall.
Under these lights allowing no shadows
our fugitive and cloistered virtue

cannot tell danger from peril,
mistakes what lounges in newsprint
for what beckons from bone.

But what if this week's special
were mandrake root? Imagine
the paradise

of russets lost! These lights would buzz
like dying flies, this music choke
on its own lid.

Down what dim, strange aisles
we might race a wayward cart.

The Conscientious Objector's Annual Memorial at the Public Library

in memory of William Stafford

It helps to remember your eye only.
      Soft sphere in that hollow
            scooped from bone.

Your kaleidoscope iris: broken glass
      shifting after pattern.
            Cornea:

pane clear and shimmering as sudden rain
      on a hot summer street.
            The slow float

of your vitreous humor. When you went
      for your driver's license,
            that eye chart—

did its letters start large and still, then fall
      as coils inscrutable
            with writhing?

When the clerk called, "Enough," did you zigzag
      down that pit? Did you flirt
            with venom,

translate snake after snake into signal?
      Such prophecy, and yet—
            such burden.

Today, as we heft and honor your task,
      we Braille our present state
            of blindness.

The Conscientious Objector's Annual Memorial
at the Public Library

after Neruda

You rise from water wrinkled and heaped upon
yourself. I shake you from your embarrassment,
coax you from folding over your many, many
private parts. I keep you damp and limp
with droplets, spread you like our planet's skin
and smooth the whitecap creases from your seas,
my chapped hands moving, moving. I iron out
the profane from all your sacred surfaces.
I hang you up to rest, to consider land
too dry for anything but olive trees.

Each new day, hands like mine create and shape
the world anew. Electric fire unites
with steel as linens for tables, bodies, beds—
fresh from their skirmishes with heartless washtubs—
seek me for solace. Your purity returns
from foam and lather. I take you up blank-white,
ready for holy pressing. I steam to life
your dove within and urge her to fly off,
to seek dry land, smooth-feathered and alone.

Explaining Black Holes to a Downy Woodpecker in January with
Help from John Cage's 4' 33"

Yes, she's refilled the suet basket with you
and yours in mind for this record spell of ice.
When you found it empty yesterday, perhaps . . .
it only seemed so? And perhaps you thought, *Is this*
what the human caged in glass means by "black holes"?

Well, she did not mean spots on retinas
or a rift draining vigor from a marriage.
Perhaps you sensed she meant a gravity
so strong it tugs away the wholesome fat
and seeds that cede survival these cold days?
No. She's read that stars conclude their lives
as blackened gaps, while you and she will shrink
to feather, bone, or ash. She dimly grasps
the mathematical model that projects
the star's final throb of light before the black.

As it blinks out, that star might sense how iron
formed at its core, a mass to collapse as fuel
burns off—though stars ignore the gravity
of the situation, overlook the curve
of space where hungers, questions, intersect.

While you've fed, she's played John Cage for you:
four minutes, thirty-odd seconds of silence
and heartbeat—hers—while time enfolds you both.
In what is left of ambient grace and sound,
join her in shutting out all sense of this:
how your two comet trails cross where rendered fat
of slaughtered cows congeals as a galaxy
of embryonic worlds to lose, devour.

Botticelli's Venus in Later Life

1

You never think to question how I'm posed.
What mollusk gave its life so I could raft
on its shell, above the waters of my birth?
I'm naked but for the hank of haunch-length hair
with which my hand and arm—so oddly hinged—
contrive to hide my pubis, as the age
required. I wonder: is it the spectacle
that draws you in? Two Zephyrs in human form
blow me dry. Lips pursed, cheeks puffed, the male
sports wings. To keep aloft, the wingless female
clings to him (as women should or must?).
From this airy pair, spring flowerlets waft my way.
Likewise sprigged are the gown the Hora wears
and the cape she offers me. This is the point
where (nubile, pliant) I end my tale for you.

2

News flash: my After clashes with Before.
Once immortals left me to my fate,
birds—six swan-geese—came to my defense.
They goosed me: "Shed that robe of servitude!"
I donned a fire-red gown of mutiny
as they haloed me and squawked of where to find
those folklore realms where risk and turmoil lurk—
where the pulse pumps, eager to seek thorned paths.
Their invitation pledged that I could win—
or lose—depending on my will and wit.
While you weren't looking, that's the life I chose.
Out of your control, I'm in my own.
Now nothing's hidden by my sultry hair.
Disheveled, skipping through summer, trading spring
for fall—I dare winter to do its worst.

21st Century Wife of Bath Comes across Six-Legged Sex:
The Erotic Lives of Bugs

Calling all leg men—leg women as well.
Consider all that you might do with *six*!
Triple your pair's agility? *Oh my!*

Think how strong a grasshopper's haunch appears.
Picture the rainbow frog beetle's hind pair
at the gym—in aqua Spandex workout-togs.
If tattoos thrill you, certain insects sport
tats so intricate, rain-forest tribes
paint the harlequin beetle's on their shields.

Perhaps such warriors admire as well the male's
vastly extended forelegs, thought (it says
right here) "to help subdue a female."
            The hell,
you say! Sucks worse than mosquitoes! Count me out
and count me down—back down—in legs, to two.

Frau Karl Marx Writes Home for Money

30 April 1855
28 Dean Street
London

Brother, you will say I ask too soon
after your last generosity—
will say I owe you explanations
before I sink to begging again.
Here they are, the answers you paid for.

Do you practice necessary economies?
I practice many. Some will shame you.
I suckled little Föxchen myself—
an English wet nurse too expensive.
He worked so fiercely at my breasts,
they broke open, blood dyeing his cheek.

Can it truly be so desperate?
Winter night, the rent late. Two bailiffs
seize linens, beds, even the cradle.
We lay on bare floor, my children cold.
Back then, I did not press you much.
I do so now, three small coffins later.

Cannot your husband find gainful employment?
He writes each day at the Reading Room.
Says the path home through public houses
is full of minds, their education
not cheap. My husband's cause galls you both—
it plagues his spine with boils huge as fists.

Can he not "study" to have fewer children?
Ferdinand, do you mean to chide me
for the ones left? Or our servant-girl's
mischance? That one's gone to a childless
couple and no further expense. Please—
Brother!—never again scrape that wound.

On Good Friday, my beloved Musch
died in his father's arms. My sons gone,
I kneel before you, girls at my skirts.
While you men sweat out words to save us,
we go on with the small tasks: cabbages,

brooms, a hand at fevered midnight.
Brother, feeding your nieces will not
also feed their father's work. For all
that divides you, one view you both share
is how we, your females, pose no danger.

Mrs. Wold Writes a Friend in North Dakota

Tomorrow, my reckoning with eighty.
At the first shriek in my joints
I will rise to walk the lane
as far as the new intersection
where tires whine through rain
and dry the pavement out of season.

I came to Oregon a prairie girl.
Sixty years of Douglas fir
have not forested my blood.
For you, late October arcs blue
over plains penciled with stubble.
Sun and snow promise sharp relief.

Here, my birthday falls with leaves
not content to blaze and vanish.
Pockets of blackberry go limp with rain
and cling with no shame through spring.
Clouds rob the winter of distinctions
the shadows would keep in stock.

The young do not worship weather
and are not permitted to hear
her prophecies that our old bones
confide to one another.
The young believe our senses fail—
I tell you, they conspire!

I now hear every neighborhood Goth
who plunders my walnut trees.
I can smell the blackberry vines' plot
to take the south fence next spring.
I have tasted loneliness and solitude
and know which to keep in my cupboard.

From my window I no longer read
the red whims of my mailbox flag.
Yet I can translate each line
chanted by the distant skeletons
of frame houses circling the spot
where Strom's barn still stood last May.

Let me tell you about tomorrow.
At twilight I slice the cake
and compliments of my annual visitors.
Nothing I say will free children
nailed by parents to chairs.
Forks will scuttle after crumbs.

I will dig from tissue this year's teacup.
I will hold to light its saucer
as though old prayers were answered there.

Translator's Notes on the Isle of Unst's Norn Fragment,
Förkortning Saga

Don't let the umlaut throw you.
ö is an O is a mouth telling a tale.
Though how the Swedish alphabet ensnared
this Shetland text remains a mystery.
That aside, our tale starts at the sea.
Something about seals? How grey seals are—quote—
common as flies on a salmon carcass—unquote?
Or could this translate to something like *to pause*
to watch so common a sight as seals is foolish
as watching houseflies? Foolish, when you need
to work at cutting peat, if "Peder" here
could mean *Peat Cutter*, not *Berserker Pete*.
Then we have an idler who neglects the fuel
for fighting Nordic chill once days grow short
and rousing yarns bind men to the great hall.

Time and damp devoured
what's next, though we can speculate that here
our obligatory hero shows his face.
Who else would mouth (would "O") the ensuing rant
against the slipshod values of his day?
Who else would, kenning after kenning, mourn
(*ubi sunt*) for a lost golden age?
Rather, for the *pewter days of yore.*
Or is this *smelter days*? A jarring note
if what we seek is epic without the drear
that grimes and grays our post-industrial day—
if what we seek from the past is certainty.
Indecision pocks our scholarship:

do we go with *pewter*? *smelter*? something *smelt*?
Or *smelt*, the fish, the salmon's textual link?

The hero's journey halts
fifty lines on, the next hide's lost to bog
and slime. Yes, hides: this tale was stained
on heavy parchment made from aurochs skins,
with aurochs-runes fringing all text, cut deep
in the short-twig style we also call Rök runes—
another umlaut. *ö* is an O is a mouth
telling the tale that here breaks off, its trail
destroyed, eroded by catastrophes
not of our making: microbes, bad luck, rot.

Here our conviction falters yet again.
We circle back to what we thought we dodged:
uncertainty, the housefly of our age.

If we're to close the books
(rather, to close this pile of moldered hides),
we must devise heroics of our own
to elude the flaws and fly-specks of *perhaps*.
We must take up the role of mouth (the O)
and claim the task of filling in all holes
with what we seek in our own age and lives.
Translation? Transmutation? The difference?
We always read ourselves. This is the need
we never name in all our showy jargon.
We mine such texts for anything it takes

to tell ourselves we're not parenthetical
(we're neither salmon carcass nor its flies)
and yet might carve Valhalla in our tales.

Mrs. Wold Writes a Friend in North Dakota

for Laura Weeks, poet and Russian Romantics buff

He exhausts me. Not for the usual reason.
Tiresome, how I must goose him toward his goal.
The list of triggers required by his contraption!
He needs to call me "Fairy," "Angel," "Sprite."
Then I must twinkle, glow, or wink the part.

Vaseline dabbed into my eyes achieves
the glazed and fathomless gaze he needs to melt
as butter in his skillet, a sizzling blur.
Once, I forgot to wear azure and gold,
colors that light his candle. It flickered out.

Those Ikea tags I failed to snip from sheets?
He claims he never recovered—lost a poem
he'd slavered for. My restive shoes hiked here,
where coffee-grinder rumpus cannot fray
his neurons bundled like sheaves against the wind.

This Sumatra brew I sip: its whiff of earth
gives respite from my airy tedium.
Nothing new in the classifieds today.
This job must serve until something—someone!—
better, less rapacious, comes my way.

The Dance Instructor Steels Himself for the Upcoming Class, or Why I Hate the Villanelle

Embrace each partner though you loathe the dance
Honor all notes whether crooned or skirled.
In the tedium of steps, seek variance.

When your students seem a conga line of ants,
picture how a nautilus shell is whorled
and embrace your partner though you loathe the dance.

Lose yourself in rhythm: seize your chance
to find routine fresh when it's next unfurled.
Convince yourself there's hope for variance.

Most of all, exude exuberance:
make sure each client's amply clutched and twirled.
Embrace that partner though you loathe the dance.

Think of gazelles and not of elephants
or trampled feet, those hazards in a world
where pattern's bruised by too much variance

in this form you feign to love so that it enchants
those who never guess, as they're waltzed and whirled,
you embrace your partner—though you loathe the dance—
and serve what's expected, with paltry variance.

Korea, Dano Festival: A Final Cautionary Tale

Cork squares topped with spring
scenes by eighteenth-century master
Shin Yun-bok.
Souvenirs from a place and time
you'll never see or know:
coasters to catch chilled sweat
of tumblers caging ice.

A woman glides on a swing
along a brush-stroked stream
where women wash their hair.
The one whose braids reach
her knees? She needs a growling dog
to warn her: young monks crouch
behind that boulder, men who leer
when loosened gowns reveal breasts.

What of this will you remember?
You embrace your shivering flesh,
the stream so cold, your sodden braids
so heavy down your spine.
At your breastbone, ties loosen.
Silk slips off one shoulder.
A dog barks, lopes your way,
your dog now.

Uncollected Poems

Dear John Letter

Hey, it's me—the grit in your oyster that never turned
to pearl—writing to you, cigarette butt in my salad
before I finished lunch. Whatthehell were you doing
in last night's storm, knocking at my dream door
after all these years of leaving me alone,
in peace? Was it because your new wife phoned, edgy,
quavering, duty-bound to share your news?
I slipped into my *better-you-than-I* apron
and served her alas sandwiches of *ooh* and *ah*,
with a side of pardon, free of charge. My dream door,
back to that—what was your point in tracking mud
to its welcome mat with nothing new to *tsk* or *blub*?
And why did we pretend that you still lived?

THE DRY FACTS

The lion is the only social cat,
a feline groupie. The rest are solo acts:
puma, ocelot, our house cats, too,
unless we force them into doggy packs
against their nature, and call this *family*.

THE WET FACTS

Cats in ancient Egypt plied the Nile,
retrievers of small fowl arrowed down.
Cats don't hate water if it's warm enough.
A catpaw rumpus! as Turkish van-cats swim
to court the charity of fishing boats.

CONCLUSIONS

. . . are not the point if you're still fixed on cats,
still sift for signs through sand or litter box.
The point you seek is what you have learned of *you*?
Pack animal or solitary beast
licking traces of the past from paws?

Shall I list what you kept from me? Shade,
a tree's defining grace. Telling time
by sun. Far horizons, rarely seen.
Sunsets denied me as you brooded,
hunched along the sea's west wall, then rolled
ashore before sun could fingerpaint
its sky. Your sodden, taciturn funks!
I left. Hooked up with effusive rain.

Last night you lurked outside my window,
slipping the moon in and out of your
pocket, like a coin you couldn't spend.
Rain is out of town this week. So where's
the harm in chatting over a cup
of tea? Jasmine Yin Hao. For you, haze
and fumes. For me, blooms you never let
me grow behind the redwood curtain.

My twice—boiled rancor's gone flat. Is it
time to switch to Earl Grey? Bergamot.
Pert citrus speaking up for itself.

An audience of two, we learn the stars,
King Time and Lady Solitude, prepare
for their act by feasting on the off-stage arm
of Grace, Professor Runestave's willing wife.

Twelve-inch, one-ring show. Three nameless fleas,
wired upside-down, are juggling cotton wads.
The magnifying glass we're urged to use
(to prove the fleas are real and not a trick
of charlatan mechanics) reveals this feat
is each flea's vain attempt to flee its ball,
ten times its size, in search of Grace and blood.
Each tiny Atlas spins aloft his world
until it's time for tape-recorded fanfare
to toot and tout the pending main event.

A hanky-curtain parts, and there's King Time
wearing a spangle crimpled as a crown.
He's hitched before a minute cart and flanked
by a pair of unnamed fleas who aid his task.
"Time's wingèd chariot has come to this?"
I whisper, marveling at the tiny wheels,
how they spin on unseen axles, acts of faith,
in Time's uneven crawl from the flashlight's glare
that lifts to filigree-harnessed Solitude
fastened to her high-wire of worsted yarn.
A black pen urges her forward—and creep
she does, in this solo act that mirrors her name.

I leave the tent
      alone.
      Wince in the glare
of the hot Tucson spring that rushes pulse.
Hands fret at making shade for eyes that need
to flee—cast off—the blinding ball of time.

Why the Field Guide Squirrels of the West *Avoids the Word "Rodent"*

Simple neglect? Perhaps. Intelligent
design? Less likely. Association quiz:
take the word "rat"—what does it call to mind?
Plague? Filth? Now this one: "chipmunk"? Comic? pert?
When we consider matters *Rodentia*,
we never speak of *lovely* or *revered*.
(I knew a marmot *lovely* in her bones?)

And speaking of bones:
this field guide gives two ways—just two—to tell
the Allen's chipmunk from the yellow-cheeked,
Townsend's, or Siskiyou. You need to know
each cry "intimately." Or, scrutinize
each penis bone—a step requiring death.

And speaking of intimately (intimacy):
how can we feel alone once rodents chew
through wiring under houses or hoods of cars?
One violation's heard, the other's not,
yet both gnaw morsel-solitude to crumbs.

And speaking of wiring:
how can we feel secluded when we're wired
to each slight *scritch* in hollow walls at night,
proof we have company and aren't alone?

And speaking of walls:
how can we get them back as barriers
once rodents gnaw our solitude away?
Seek the scent of lemon verbena leaves
crushed on solitary walks at dusk?

And speaking of solitude,
natural enemy of loneliness:
both states are natural prey of rodents—rat,
mouse, marmot, chipmunk, capybara, squirrel—
all whose incisors never stop their growth
and must gnaw nuts or seeds or wires or walls.

And speaking of squirrels:
might I spend a second life as one who flies?
A Northern? Eyes: huge marbles, midnight black.
I want its glide membranes, thin flaps of flesh
to swag from limbs now known as arms and legs.
By the grace of overlapping DNA,
if squirrels would let me join in such a state
I vow to nibble anything they say.

Four Definitions for the Use of Time

1
Your book club neighbor chats across the fence
of marginalia you'd feel rude to halt.
You're late for the doctor's bad news redefining
late as good. (Here, time as minutes saved
before the clock's face and hands tic with fear.)

2
Our dead forget all of their favorite colors
but not how we felt when our red wine stained
their table's open grain. (Time as rebuke,
selective as trout hungry for nymphs,
and you with nothing but dry flies to pimp.)

3
The lawn defines itself once grass aligns
with like shades cordoned off from random greens.
(Linear pas*time*, two deft steps to where
Aristotle applauds your logic's genus,
differentia, and cool distraction.)

4
The ER doctor said the midnight skunk
saved your life. Its stench woke you in time.
(Here, a temporal housemaid scours grit
from crisis, rasps and files time's rough, chipped edge—
though if chafed too long, the fault fissures anew.)

Coda
Consider circles in dreams that make you sweat:
those rubber loops back to unfinished grief.
That pain, like time, is useful for its waste.

Bring old clothes. Pack shirts, their seams mended
beneath arms you take care not to raise,
their frayed cuffs turned under with less shame
each time. Take along knits unraveling
near seams, stitch by stitch, like the mind
loosens toward sleep. Pack slacks with flanks
flecked in blood the wash failed to fade
or to help you forget. The plan?
At the next fresh stain, you'll shed
its garment on the rented
bed of the brief city
where the body lingers zipped
tight in self-importance
even as the mind slips
from its patched overcoat.
Next, lighten the suitcase
so it holds nothing
but the boarding pass
for the last flight out.
Let its straps go slack
from the lack of
purpose, its lock
easing open
like a mouth
with nothing
more to
mourn.

Carolyn Moore (1944–2019) was the author of four chapbooks—*Against a Second Fall*, winner of the New Eden Chapbook Prize; *The Great Uncluttering*, winner of the Bread and Lightning Chapbook Competition; *The Flavors of Quarks and Blame*, winner of the Refined Savage Press National Poetry Competition; and *The Seven Deadlies*, winner of *Interrobang*'s Chapbook Competition—and one full-length collection, *What Euclid's Third Axiom Neglects to Mention about Circles* (White Pine Press, 2013). In total, Moore won over 60 awards and honors for her writing, including the New Millennium Writing Award, the Foley Poetry Award, and the C. Hamilton Bailey Fellowship from Literary Arts. She taught literature and creative writing at Humboldt State University in Arcata, California, before returning to Oregon to work as a freelance writer on the last vestige of the family farm in Tigard. Legacy was very important to Moore, and in 2019, her desire to see her estate become a center of learning and poetry was realized in Portland Community College's Carolyn Moore Writing Residency.